Festivals *of the* *World*

BRAZIL

TIMES EDITIONS

Written by
SUSAN MCKAY

Designed by
LOO CHUAN MING

Picture research by
SUSAN JANE MANUEL

© **TIMES EDITIONS PTE LTD 1997**
Originated and designed by
Times Books International
an imprint of Times Editions Pte Ltd
Times Center, 1 New Industrial Road
Singapore 536196
Tel: 2848844
Fax: 2854871

Printed in Singapore

ISBN 981 204 752 2

CONTENTS

It's Festival Time . . .

The Portuguese word for "festival" is *festa* [FESS-ta], but Brazilian festivals come from a mixture of different traditions—European, African, and Amazon Indian. Over the years these festivals have changed as more and more new people have come to Brazil. So come along and add your own special something to the celebrations. It's festa time in Brazil…

WHERE'S BRAZIL?

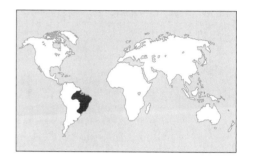

Brazil is the largest country in **Latin America**. In fact, it covers almost half of the continent of South America. The main feature of the country is the Amazon River. The Amazon River is the second longest river in the world after the Nile River in Africa.

Brazilians are a mix of many different cultures and backgrounds.

Who are the Brazilians?

When explorers came to Brazil from Portugal in 1500, they found groups of Indians living in the Amazon rain forest. The Portuguese only began to settle in Brazil 30 years later. They started huge sugar plantations but they didn't have enough people to work on them. Slave traders captured people from West Africa and brought them across the ocean to work as slaves. More recently, in the mid-1900s, immigrants came from Japan and Europe. Today, all these different people live together in Brazil.

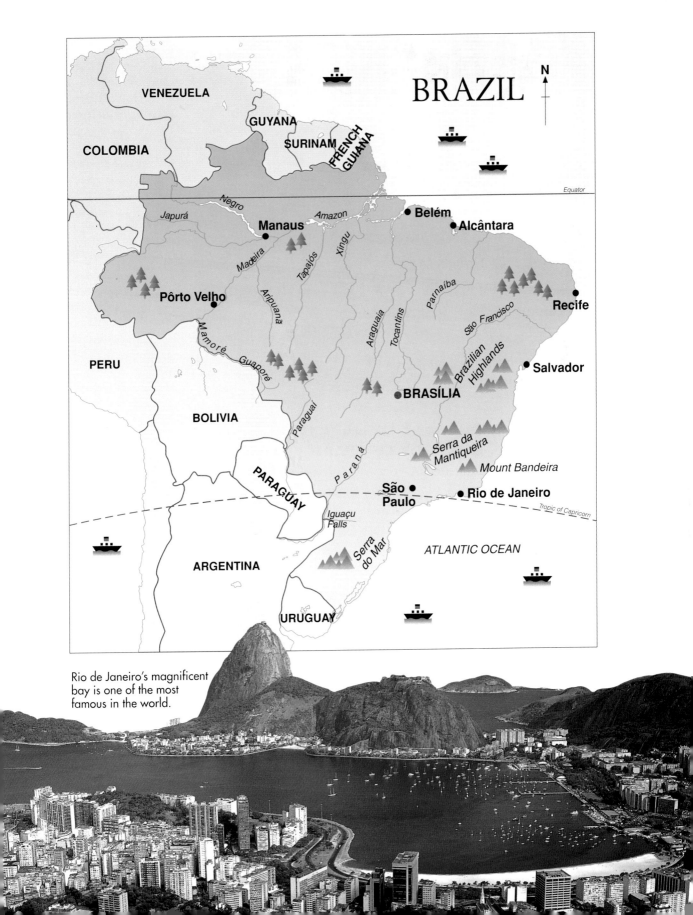

BRAZIL

N

VENEZUELA

COLOMBIA

GUYANA

SURINAM

FRENCH GUIANA

Equator

Japurá

Negro

Amazon

Manaus

Belém

Alcântara

Madeira

Tapajós

Xingu

Pôrto Velho

Aripuanã

Parnaíba

Recife

Mamoré

Guaporé

Araguaia

Tocantins

São Francisco

PERU

Salvador

BOLIVIA

Paraguai

BRASÍLIA

Brazilian Highlands

Paraná

Serra da Mantiqueira

Mount Bandeira

PARAGUAY

São Paulo

Rio de Janeiro

Tropic of Capricorn

Iguaçu Falls

Serra do Mar

ATLANTIC OCEAN

ARGENTINA

URUGUAY

Rio de Janeiro's magnificent bay is one of the most famous in the world.

WHEN'S THE FESTA?

Most of Brazil lies in the Southern Hemisphere—the half of Earth that is below the equator. In the Southern Hemisphere, the seasons are exactly opposite to what they are in the Northern Hemisphere. So when it is spring in North America it is autumn in South America, and when the temperatures begin to drop in the north, they begin to rise in the south.

SPRING

- ✪ **OUR LADY OF NAZARE**
- ✪ **OUR LADY OF APARECIDA**—People make pilgrimages to the Aparecida shrine to honor a statue of the Virgin Mary that was pulled out of the river by fishermen in 1717.
  - ✪ **FESTA DA LUZ** ✪ **ESPITO SANTO**

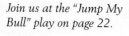
Join us at the "Jump My Bull" play on page 22.

SUMMER

- ✪ **CHRISTMAS** ✪ **LORD JESUS OF SEAFARERS**
- ✪ **YEMANJÁ** ✪ **CARNIVAL**
- ✪ **BOA VIAGEM**—Festival in honor of Our Lady of Seafarers. A procession of decorated boats transports the image of Our Lady to the port. Then she is given to the sailors, who carry her to the church to be blessed.
- ✪ **BONFIM**—Women from the state of Bahia wear beautiful costumes and wash the steps of the church of Our Lord of Good Ending (Bonfim).
- ✪ **SAINT SEBASTIAN'S DAY**—This saint's day is celebrated with processions and fireworks.

AUTUMN

⭐ **SAINT JOSÉ'S DAY** ⭐ **HOLY WEEK**—Holy Week is celebrated with processions and a famous passion play performed throughout Brazil.

⭐ **PERSIMMON FESTIVAL** ⭐ **FESTA DO DIVINO**

⭐ **BELÉM**—This festival in the city of Belém honors all the special saints who do not have feast days of their own. A procession through the streets ends at the church where fireworks are displayed.

WINTER

⭐ **SAINT ANTHONY'S DAY**

⭐ **SAINT JOHN'S DAY**

⭐ **SAINT PETER'S DAY**—Widows honor Saint Peter by placing lit candles on their doorsteps. Others enjoy the food, drink, dancing, and fireworks throughout the day.

⭐ **FESTA DE PIRAPORA**—Cities and towns hold fairs and dances to celebrate this day.

⭐ **OUR LADY OF SEAFARERS**—A water pageant is put on by sailors in the southern part of the state of São Paulo to honor Our Lady.

⭐ **AGUAS DE OXALÁ**—Followers of Candomblé undergo a purification ritual on this day.

Keep on marching to the next page for Carnival.

7

CARNIVAL

At the beginning of February, the entire country is taken by storm with singing, dancing, and merry-making. Preparations for Carnival begin months ahead of time—designing costumes and making decorations to hang in the streets. Strict Christians also prepare because after Carnival they must **fast** for 40 days to remind themselves of Christ's suffering. Traditionally, Carnival was the last time before Easter that people could eat, drink, sing, and dance to their hearts' content.

Members of samba schools rehearse all year to prepare for the big day. They wear matching costumes and execute fantastic dance steps in perfect time.

Samba schools

Carnival was originally introduced by Portuguese settlers, but over the years Brazilians have made it a festival of their own. The African contribution was samba schools. The first samba school was started by a group of black musicians in 1928. Since then, samba school parades have become the main attraction at Carnival.

Each school has about 3,000–5,000 members. To participate in the parade, the members must decide on a theme. Themes can range from events in history to famous personalities and legends. The costumes, songs, and floats are also carefully arranged to fit the theme. On the special day of the parade, the samba schools compete with one another for the grand prize.

Samba schools began in Brazil's poorest communities. Some people had to save up all year just to buy their costume. Today, rich, poor, black, brown, and white all take part in samba parades.

King Momo is Brazil's Carnival mascot. In big cities, the mayor hands over the key to the city to King Momo for the duration of the Carnival celebration.

The bateria

Two drummers get caught up in the fun at Carnival.

The **bateria** [ba-TAY-ree-a] are the percussion bands that take to the streets during the parades. The pounding of the drums and thumping of the tambourines are so loud that you can feel the vibrations through the soles of your feet. The rhythm is so strong that even if you tried you would find it hard not to join in the dancing. Soon there is a tidal wave of people filling the streets, and you are swept along with the crowd.

Music is one of the most important parts of Carnival. Songs composed for Carnival in earlier years have become hits around the world. Some samba schools work on their songs for years for a chance to compete at the Municipal Theater in Rio de Janeiro. Some of the most popular Carnival songs are naughty limericks that have been put to music.

Think about this
When Carnival was first celebrated in Brazil, the highlight of the festival was **entrudo** [en-TRUE-do]. Entrudo was a prank; festival-goers threw water, flour, and face powder at each other until they were completely unrecognizable.

YEMANJÁ

New Year's Eve is a very special day in Brazil. Not only is it the time when Brazilians usher in a new year, it is also the festival of Yemanjá, the Candomblé goddess of the sea.

On December 31st, Rio de Janeiro's famous Copacabana Beach is overrun by as many as two million people celebrating and worshiping the goddess. According to popular belief, if Yemanjá is offered gifts on her special day, she will bring prosperity to the people of the area, and a good fishing season to Brazil's many fishers. Some of her most loyal devotees are people who make their living from the sea.

Young and old, black and white worship Yemanjá. Dressed from head to foot in white, this girl would have gone through a special bathing ceremony before offering the goddess flowers.

Candomblé

Candomblé [can-DOME-blay] is the name of the religious tradition that was brought to Brazil by slaves from Nigeria and Benin. During the time of slavery in Brazil, masters prohibited their slaves from practicing Candomblé. They forced the slaves to go to church and to practice Catholicism. To keep their masters happy, the slaves pretended to worship the Christian saints when in fact they were honoring their own gods. Each Christian saint had been coupled with a Candomblé *orixa* [o-RICK-sa]. For example, Oxalá, the god of harvest, was coupled with Jesus, and Yemanjá with the Virgin Mary. After the abolition of slavery, blacks were able to worship freely, and Candomblé became widespread. Today, it is no longer a religion exclusively for Brazil's blacks.

Praying to the sea goddess is serious business. Devotees must follow strict rules before making their offerings.

People throw flowers into the water for good luck. If the flowers are carried out to sea, it will be a good year. If they come back to shore, Yemanjá is not happy with the giver.

Getting ready for the big night

Lighting candles to honor Yemanjá.

Several days before the end of the year, workers begin setting up stages on the sand. This is where the bands will perform to the millions of people who have come to celebrate the New Year. The beach is lined with huge banks of loudspeakers so the music can be heard from one end to the other.

Worshipers must make preparations as well. They will go to the stores to buy long wooden boats painted blue and white, the colors of the goddess. Later, the boats will be filled with food, combs, make-up, and mirrors because Yemanjá is said to be a very beautiful woman who loves to look at herself in the mirror.

Opposite: Fireworks light the sky at the stroke of midnight.

Bringing in the New Year

When the clock strikes midnight, everyone begins to shout "Feliz Ano Novo," Happy New Year! Blasts from horns and sirens fill the night, and firecrackers can be heard exploding from every direction. Soon the music starts up, and the dancing begins. Samba bands stroll up and down the beach entertaining the people. Everywhere you can see small candles outlining the offerings to Yemanjá so they are not trampled on by the enthusiastic dancers.

Some bands continue playing right into New Year's Day until the last of the dancers has gone home.

Think about this
January 1st is also the Day of Universal Brotherhood. Why might this day be of particular importance to Brazilians?

FESTA DO DIVINO

Just before Pentecost Sunday (50 days after Easter), towns and cities all over Brazil celebrate Festa do Divino, the Feast of the Holy Ghost. In the Christian tradition, Pentecost commemorates the sending of the Holy Spirit to the first apostles. In this country, however, Brazilians have many special ways to mark this festive occasion.

People of all ages take part in the procession for Festa do Divino.

Dress up party

In the colonial-era towns of Alcântara and Paraty, the townspeople dress in clothes dating back to the 16th century. Some people dress as famous figures in Brazilian history. Musicians stroll through the streets serenading the crowds. Finally the procession that everyone has been waiting for begins. The procession marks the arrival of the emperor. In a grand gesture to the people who have gathered to greet him, he releases all the prisoners from the town jail.

For the rest of the day, the celebrations continue in the streets with folk dramas, music, and plenty of dancing.

This woman is dressed to play the part of the empress.

The fishers' feast

Musicians form two lines at the head of the procession.

For the fishers living on the coast of Brazil, an entirely different tradition takes place at Pentecost. On this day, all the fishers dress in white from head to foot with colorful sashes and hats and carry an oar in one hand. The fishers form two lines and march through the streets in a procession toward the water. The townspeople follow while the musicians keep rhythm with the marching.

The water's edge is crammed with boats that have been decorated with brightly colored streamers and confetti. As the boats glide through the water, the fishers stand holding their oars up to the sky. Their destination is the local parish church. At the church, the sailors present their oars to the priest to be blessed for the coming year.

Capoeira

Once the processions are over, the festivities spill out into the streets where church groups organize bazaars and flea markets. Stalls line the sidewalks, selling all kinds of delicious Brazilian foods. In some areas, people perform *capoeira* [ca-po-AY-ra].

If you were to ask a Brazilian what capoeira is, he or she would have trouble answering you. This is because capoeira falls into a category somewhere between martial arts and dance. When capoeira was first brought to Brazil by Angolan slaves, it was a type of foot-fighting. In Brazil, if slaves were caught fighting by their owners, both sides were punished. Since fighting was the only way they had of resolving their differences, they had to disguise it as a dance with musical accompaniment.

Over the years, capoeira has been refined. Today, you can see it on nearly every street corner in Brazil, especially during festivals. Contestants are only allowed to use their legs, heels, feet, and heads to deliver blows to their opponent's body. They do this by moving across the floor in a series of handstands and cartwheels.

Left and opposite: Brazil is often called a country of rhythm. This is because percussion instruments, such as the drum and the tambourine, are the most essential parts of any Brazilian band.

The **berimbau** [bay-reem-BOW], seen here in the background, is the most common instrument used for capoeira. It is shaped like a bow with a metal wire running from the top to the bottom. The base of the instrument is filled with seeds to make a shaker, while the single string is played with a copper coin.

Think about this

The early colonists thought African music and dance traditions were obscene. But many African slaves were very talented musicians. By the 1800s, African instruments, such as the berimbau, were mainstream. Today, they form the backbone of Brazilian music.

SAINT JOHN'S DAY

Every day seems like a festival day in June. Just after Pentecost ends, a new cycle of festivals begins, lasting throughout the month of June. This is because the feast days for Saint John, Saint Anthony, and Saint Peter all fall in June. While Saints Peter and Anthony's days are celebrated quietly at church, the streets of cities and towns all across Brazil come alive on Saint John's Day with music, fireworks, and brightly lit giant balloons that fill the sky and blaze through the night.

In the big cities, people dress up as *caipiras* [kye-PEE-ras], or country bumpkins, and take part in square dances to celebrate Saint John's Day.

Left: Country and western is the theme for Saint John's Day. Even the musicians wear cowboy hats.

Opposite: Giant balloons spot the sky on the night of the festival.

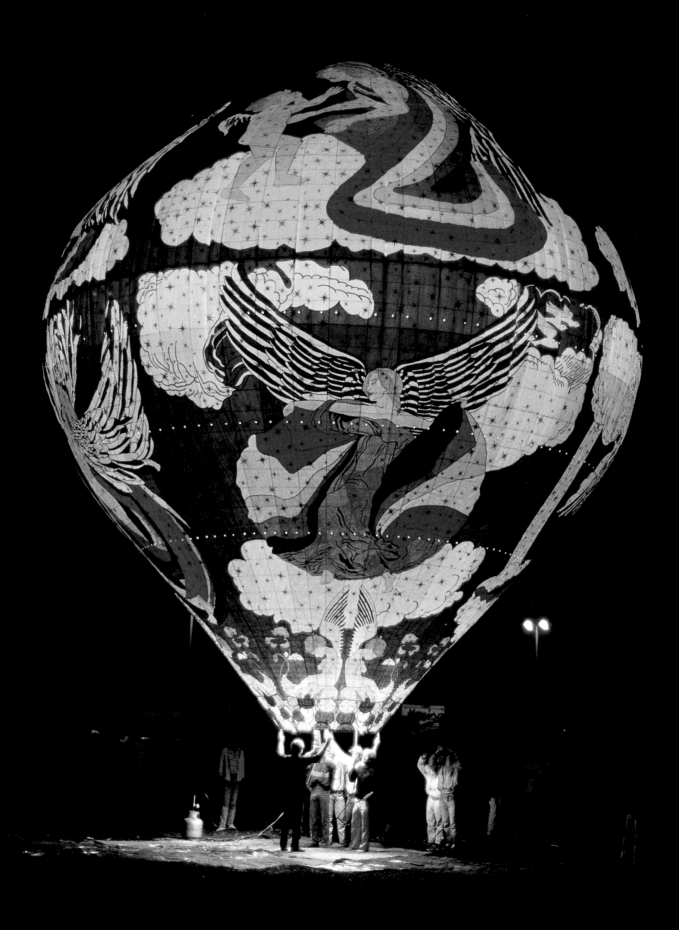

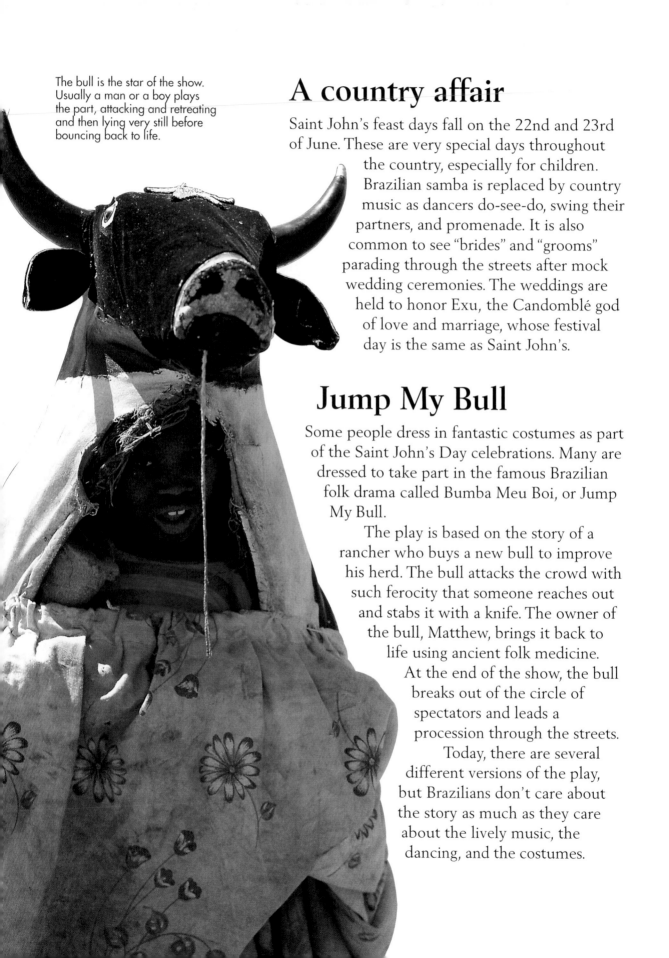

The bull is the star of the show. Usually a man or a boy plays the part, attacking and retreating and then lying very still before bouncing back to life.

A country affair

Saint John's feast days fall on the 22nd and 23rd of June. These are very special days throughout the country, especially for children. Brazilian samba is replaced by country music as dancers do-see-do, swing their partners, and promenade. It is also common to see "brides" and "grooms" parading through the streets after mock wedding ceremonies. The weddings are held to honor Exu, the Candomblé god of love and marriage, whose festival day is the same as Saint John's.

Jump My Bull

Some people dress in fantastic costumes as part of the Saint John's Day celebrations. Many are dressed to take part in the famous Brazilian folk drama called Bumba Meu Boi, or Jump My Bull.

The play is based on the story of a rancher who buys a new bull to improve his herd. The bull attacks the crowd with such ferocity that someone reaches out and stabs it with a knife. The owner of the bull, Matthew, brings it back to life using ancient folk medicine.

At the end of the show, the bull breaks out of the circle of spectators and leads a procession through the streets. Today, there are several different versions of the play, but Brazilians don't care about the story as much as they care about the lively music, the dancing, and the costumes.

The dancers are accompanied by a band of musicians who play a rhythmic beat. During the course of the play, they may call out to the other actors to get a laugh from the audience.

This man is playing the part of the *vaqueiro* [va-CAY-ro], the cowboy.

Think about this

Some people believe Bumba Meu Boi is a parody of the bullfights that once took place in Portugal. In those bullfights, the **matador** only pretended to kill the bull. Once the crowd was quiet, the bull would jump back up and surprise them.

CAYAPO FESTIVALS

After the settlers from Portugal came to Brazil, things changed for many of the Amazon Indians, especially the Cayapo. They were moved from their land to large reservations. Most Cayapo adopted modern housing and clothing. Today, some of their ancient traditions are being revived to remind the people of their roots. One of the most popular traditions is Cayapo dance. These dances were once performed during festive occasions, but today they are performed to teach Brazilians the history of the Cayapo Indians.

Feather headdresses, such as these, are only worn to mark very special occasions.

Dancing

Dancing is an important part of Cayapo culture. Many years ago, dances were performed at festivals as a form of entertainment, and to protect the dancer from **supernatural** forces.

The Cayapo dance performed today is based on the story of a Cayapo boy killed during a Portuguese attack. In the dance, the medicine man and the village chief pray to God day and night until the boy comes back to life. No instruments are used. The sound of the staffs and feet pounding the dirt is the only accompaniment. The beat provides a rhythm for the story which is sung by the performers as they dance.

Body painting is an ancient tradition. Children are given special markings from the time they are a few days old, and the pattern is re-painted every 10–12 days. Most Cayapo wear modern clothing today.

Cayapo children born within a certain time frame are all considered the same age. When a group is old enough, a special ceremony is held, and the whole group moves up one grade.

25

THINGS FOR YOU TO DO

I n Brazil, one of the favorite things for children to make during Carnival is ***cascarones*** [cas-ca-ROH-ness]. Cascarones are part of the Carnival tradition of entrudo, or playing pranks on people.

What are cascarones?

Cascarones are brightly colored eggs that you crack over someone's head. But instead of a yolk, the egg is filled with bits of paper that come showering down. Sound like fun? Here's how to make them.

How to make cascarones

Ask your mother or father for an egg from the refrigerator. The first step is a little tricky, so you may want to ask for help, too. Very carefully make a hole at the small end with a needle. You will have to make the hole bigger and bigger, little by little, to be sure you can fit the confetti in the top. Pour the egg out through the hole into a bowl. Rinse the eggshell carefully and let it dry. Make confetti by cutting strips of colored paper into tiny squares. Place the confetti in the egg and seal it by gluing a piece of paper around the hole. Now decorate the outside of the egg with markers or paints and get ready to crack!

Sing a Carnival song

Once you've finished making your cascarones, here's another thing for you to do. Do you know anyone who can play the piano? If so, ask them to play this melody for you, and learn the words to a famous Carnival song, "Ciranda." Dance in a circle while you're singing it, and change direction when you reach the line that reads, "then go back the other way."

Ciranda

Things to look for in your library

The Amazon: A Young Reader's Look at the Last Frontier. Marcos Santilli and Peter Lourie (Boyd Mills Press, 1991).

Brazil: Rhythm, Music, People. (North Carolina State University, Humanities Extension Publications).

Carnavalia! African-Brazilian Folklore and Crafts. Luzi Papi (Ruzzoli Institute, 1994).

How Night Came From the Sea: A Story From Brazil. C. Golembe & Mary-Joan Gerson (Little, Brown & Co, 1994).

Meet Andre: A Brazilian Youth. (North Carolina State University, Humanities Extension Publications).

MAKE A CARNIVAL CAP

D uring Brazil's Carnival period you can see all kinds of spectacular costumes. One of the things that makes them so special are the headdresses. Here are some instructions to make your very own Carnival cap!

7

5

8

9

10

6

You will need:
1. Construction paper
2. Glue
3. A stapler
4. Feathers, sequins, glitter
5. Scissors
6. Paints
7. A paint tray
8. Paintbrushes
9. A pencil
10. Ribbon

4

2

3

1

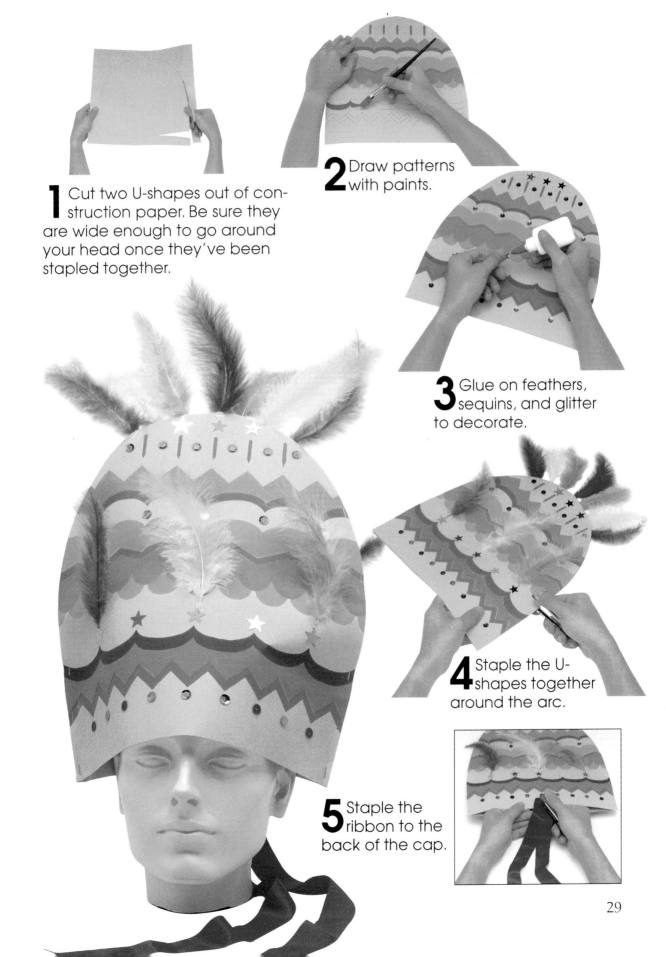

1 Cut two U-shapes out of construction paper. Be sure they are wide enough to go around your head once they've been stapled together.

2 Draw patterns with paints.

3 Glue on feathers, sequins, and glitter to decorate.

4 Staple the U-shapes together around the arc.

5 Staple the ribbon to the back of the cap.

29

MAKE COCADA BRANCA

Cocada Branca is a very sweet Brazilian dessert that tastes especially delicious when served with fruits, such as oranges and pineapple. The coconut in the recipe gives the dish a very tropical flavor.

You will need:

1. 1½ cups (180 g) grated coconut
2. ¾ cup (170 g) brown sugar
3. 1 cup (240 ml) milk
4. 4 cloves
5. A wooden spoon
6. A saucepan
7. Measuring cups

1 Bring the sugar, cloves, and milk to a boil in the saucepan.

2 Remove the saucepan from the heat and add the grated coconut. Mix well.

3 Cook on low heat for 10 minutes.

Chill in the refrigerator overnight and then dig in the next day for a treat you won't forget!

GLOSSARY

bateria, 11	The percussion bands that play during the samba school parade.
berimbau, 19	A single stringed instrument played with a copper coin.
Candomblé, 13	African religion in which followers believe they can be possessed by magical spirits.
capoeira, 18	A dance or martial art in which participants can only use their legs, feet, heels, and head to deliver blows.
cascarones, 26	Confetti-filled eggs cracked over heads during Carnival.
entrudo, 11	An old Portuguese Carnival tradition of playing pranks.
fast, 8	Eating no food for a period of time.
Latin America, 4	A region including South America, Central America, and Mexico.
matador, 23	A bullfighter.
orixa, 13	Candomblé gods.
supernatural, 25	Things that are believed to have magical powers.
vaqueiro, 23	A cowboy.

INDEX